MIRACLE PEOPLE — An Inspiring Anthology

Of Differently-Abled Beings

Copyright 2018

By Sue Snyder

ISBN 978-0-9796134-3-2

All opinions expressed in this anthology are those of the contributors and are not meant to recommend any possible treatment for physical conditions.

Miracle People: An Introduction

Around 3:00 a.m. I heard him hobbling back from the bathroom assisted by a crutch on his left, balancing himself by hanging onto the doorframes, the bathroom shelving, then grabbing his grocery cart and finally, the bedside table. As he flopped down on the bed, he grabbed his legs and swung them up and over the edge of the mattress, using his stronger left arm to yank his knees up toward his chest and rolling onto his right side. I rolled over and asked, "Are you awake?" Dumb question? Yes.

But wait. Brilliant ideas often come in the middle of the night. I needed to share my inspired thoughts about my next book. I thought the title "Struck Up" (or something like that) would be appropriate for an anthology of inspiring stories from our many friends who are "differently-abled." Richard and I began listing folks whom we thought to be coping well with their conditions and decided to ask them to share their stories and their upbeat attitudes.

Quite often people who see Richard trying to get his electric scooter (The Rascal) back into his van will ask, "Can I help?" His response is always a cheerful, "Yeah, stand by for a minute." Or "Yes, hold my crutch." Or "I got this, but don't stop asking people if they need help even if one of them grunts, 'No, I can do it myself.'" Wouldn't the world be a better place if we all asked strangers and neighbors and family and friends if they needed help?

Our friends in this book are dealing with Parkinson's, Multiple Sclerosis, Huntington's Disease, and Strokes. Some have varying degrees of blindness or birth defects or have been set back by severe accidents. Each of these people has devised ways to cope with limited and challenging conditions. Wouldn't it be wonderful if we could inspire the depressed, the newly diagnosed, those ready to just give up, with inspirational stories of folks who met their challenges, who didn't become bogged down by their "poor me" thoughts, who overcame obstacles that could have led to defeat.

When Richard and I ask the question "what keeps you going" the answers are "my wife" or "my husband" or "my dog" or "my church." They have all reached out for support, for an arm to lean on. They have all found ways to achieve peace of mind regardless of circumstances. All have risen above considering themselves as victims.

I like to quote what the Dali Lama had to say about this: "The purpose of life is happiness. The way to happiness is through service." I find it so true. We hope you enjoy getting to know these amazing beings. We are so fortunate to have them in our lives.

Love and Blessings, Sue Snyder

Dedication

These stories are dedicated to all
the Miracle People everywhere.
May you continue
to rise above circumstances and
to thrive, sometimes against
all odds.

You inspire the rest of us to live
the best lives possible and
we thank you.

Stories by Miracle People

"Where there is great love there are always miracles."

Willa Cather

A Sixth Toe

Kathryn Gill Reynolds Housden

I came into this world with my right foot having a sixth toe. The doctor who helped at my birth, tied a string around the little bit of extra skin and told my parents that this was nothing to worry about. Little did my parents know that it was a precursor to a birth defect in my right hip and right leg.

When I was three years old, my mother was giving me a bath in the sink and noticed that my right leg was one half inch shorter than my left leg. We lived in a small town, Susanville, California, and mother read in the newspaper that an orthopedic doctor was bringing a "Bone Clinic" to town. Mother took me to see him—Dr. Donald King—head of orthopedics at Stanford-Lane Hospital in San Francisco.

From that date on our family went to San Francisco every six months and Dr. King took X-rays of my hips and legs. I remember this so well because I would receive a "treat" if I was patient and was a "good girl" – we would go to the Zoo or the Japanese Tea Garden or have dinner at "The Cliff House."

I wore a built-up shoe on my right foot and I did limp, as the difference in the length of my legs grew more pronounced. I remember that I always had to have brown shoes that could have a built-up heel attached and other kids got colored footwear. And yet I could run, jump, hop and skip. I was my Dad's "SKIPPER" as we walked together with me skipping to keep up with his long strides. He was six feet, two inches in height.

In 1941, we moved to La Jolla, California, and I had the care of an orthopedic surgeon in San Diego. He operated on my right hip, trying to irritate the right hip joint to make it grow. I was in a body cast for 9 weeks, in the tiny Scripps Hospital in La Jolla. All of our family relatives sent me cards and letters and I received mail every day except two. My mother and father came to see me almost every day. I did cry very hard once when my roommate got to go home and I still had several weeks to stay in the Hospital. However, all the doctors and nurses were very kind and cheerful in caring for me.

I was thrilled when the day came for my cast to come off and four days later I got to go home. My first meal at home was "t-bone steak with mushroom gravy" and I wore a pink dress with blue buttons. I walked on crutches for twelve weeks to gain strength back into my legs. When I went back to school (in this new town), I was elected President of my third grade class. I am so fortunate that I was never teased.

When I was 9 years old, my left leg was operated on and the knee tendons were tied so that my left leg would only grow in two places just like my right leg only grew in two places. Again, I had to walk on crutches to gain strength back for walking. I could do pretty much everything and yet was nearly always chosen last to be on sports teams.

At fifteen, my last operation was done by Dr. King in San Francisco to take out three inches of my left leg femur so that it would be nearly the same length as my right leg. This time I was in the hospital for twelve weeks in a body cast and then on crutches for three months. I was taught by a "Home School Teacher" and was late starting my sophomore year of high school.

I had long scars on my legs and that made it hard to go to swimming parties during high school. I made up for that by entering into many activities and getting good grades. I also started dating in my junior year and really had many good times that year and during my senior year. Our times of fun happened in the Methodist Youth Fellowship of Friday night "good times" and Sunday night church gatherings.

After graduating from Stockton High School our family moved to the Central Valley for my father's work. I attended Fresno State College, became a kindergarten teacher, married and birthed two wonderful sons, helped to take care of my niece, and lived a pretty normal life. I loved hiking and back-packing, learned to ski and always enjoyed swimming. I was 5 foot one inch in height--all the rest of my family members are very tall. My oldest son, now 60 years old, is 6'6". It is estimated that I would have been 5'8" had my legs grown to their full length.

When I was 58 years old, my right hip was replaced at Scripps Hospital by Dr. Colwell, head of orthopedics. This hip replacement was very successful and has served me well for 25 years. I have enjoyed two long hikes in the Sierra Mountains during this time: a 50-mile, 7-day hike with UC Irvine is the first one. The second dream came true, when my second husband, Jack, helped me train for, and accompanied me, at age 67, to hike the "Yosemite Panorama Trail" from Glacier Point, 8 miles, to Happy Isles. I am so grateful for his encouragement and doing this with me.

At this time of writing, I am nearly 84 years of age. My whole right leg has become mal-formed and I need to use a walker to keep my balance when I am walking out of doors. I am filled with gratitude for:

(1) my parents who took me to see what could be   done to help this birth defect and who supported me all along the way with love and kindness;

(2) to all the orthopedic doctors who did the research for this congenital hip healing;

(3) to my Grandfather Crane who left my mother $5,000 in the 1940's to pay for these medical bills;

(4) to all the kind and patient, cheerful people who cared for me and emptied the bedpans while I was in   the body casts;

(5) and again to my parents who selected to spend   this inheritance so I would

be healthier and enjoy a   more   normal   life. There was no health insurance then.

We visited my father's birthplace of Blythedale, Missouri, and saw a boy there, about my age of 17, who had NOT been treated for the same thing. He wore an iron shoe about 8 inches tall, clamped on to his regular shoe so he could walk with one leg that was much shorter than the other. I believe he had a much different life than I was privileged to live.

I learned so many valuable spiritual characteristics: patience, kindness, compassion, humor, friendship and most of all to appreciate and treasure all that was gifted to me with great LOVE!!! And to LOVE IN RETURN!!!

"To me every hour of the light and dark is a miracle. Every cubic inch of space is a miracle."

Walt Whitman

Christina Barber-Nicolopulos

In 1980 I was concerned when I woke up with a numb foot. My brother-in-law Peter Caffee, suggested I call my neurologist, who immediately ordered a spinal tap. I was diagnosed with multiple sclerosis, a degenerative nerve disease that causes lesions in the spinal cord that can lead to all sorts of central nervous system problems, including difficulty walking and seeing.

I was scared. My doctor recommended that I avoid stress because this emotion can exacerbate symptoms. I was twenty-five and was only just beginning my career as a teacher of Spanish and Spanish-American literature. I was enrolled in a doctoral program at Harvard when I received the diagnosis. But I knew that this would require tremendous amounts of stress, precisely what my physician had warned against. I immediately withdrew from the program and transferred to Berkeley, in California, where my parents were living because I very much needed their support. What went wrong?

For mobility purposes I bought an electric scooter because my MS had reached a point that made safe driving impossible. This allowed me to continue to pursue my education classes from the renowned Argentine author, Julio Cortazar, classes covering his novels and short stories.

I am lucky to be a positive person, even when facing difficult challenges. I attribute this, in large part, to my parents who always showed me their love. My father was a kind and thoughtful person. He was a successful orthopedic surgeon, with a private practice in Berkeley, Ca. My mom was a homemaker. She and dad raised four children, one of them mentally challenged.

Right from the beginning it was clear I had mobility problems with tremendous difficulty walking. I appeared on the talk show "People are Talking" to share my experiences regarding Multiple Sclerosis with other people who were also touched by this illness. As my health improved I looked for jobs teaching Spanish at a community college and at the Pacific Lutheran Theology Seminary. When I saw an advertisement on a job board seeking a Spanish teacher at World College West, in Marin County, California, I was anxious to apply. But, unfortunately, I got a new symptom, an attack of double vision. A call to my neurologist helped calm my fears as he explained that double vision did not usually last for more than a week or two and I should definitely apply for the job.

Since I could no longer drive, I took a ferry to Marin County and then a taxi to the college. I was pleased to have made the effort but it was disconcerting to see, of all the people, the two who had interviewed me, to whom I had not mentioned my health problem for fear of jeopardizing my chances of getting the job. One month later, after a trip to Paris, I received a call from the hiring committee of World College West offering me the job. Wow! I did it, despite my physical limitations.

I was to spend three months on the Marin County campus, after which I was to drive to Mexico with the director of the program and a group of American students. I had not told the committee that I had never been to Mexico, so when I arrived I made an extra effort to familiarize myself with the people and the handicraft markets. I lived with a Mexican family who made my time in the country extra-special.

I was to drive to the villages where students were having home stays to offer moral support and get to know the families. Some of the students chose to specialize in handicrafts, such as blackstrap weaving and the making of wooden masks. The students had the extra challenge of bearing two new languages, Spanish and Parapecha, the Indian language of the state of Michoacán.

I often suffered from dizziness when I visited the villages, a symptom of my multiple sclerosis. This caused me to walk with an uneven gate, which many of the villagers concluded meant that I was a drunken borracha. "Prunic," they yelled at me. This misunderstanding is conceivable since the abuse of alcohol is common in village life.

My next challenge was to complete the Ph.D in Spanish-American Literature, which I began at Harvard in 1980. After five years, I felt able to continue my studies, so I transferred to U.C. Berkeley. The symptoms of my illness changed from a numb foot to a numb arm, to a numb leg, and finally to a numb stomach. I had very good luck with the medication Decadron to control my symptoms when I was under the stress of the doctoral program. I found swimming to be an excellent exercise for stress management. I swim routinely thirty lengths, three times a week, an activity, which builds strength in the arms and legs, and helps me to maintain positive outlook in challenging times. In recent years I inject the drug Copaxone, which has given me no side effects. It has been over 35 years that MS has been my partner. The numbness in my body has completely subsided. I continue to have difficulty walking but my battery-charged scooter has given me a remarkable amount of freedom to get around.

I am optimistic about the future. I have also been deeply in love with my boyfriend, Ken Nickoll, who loves me because of my cheerful disposition and love of life. Recently, Ken and I flew to Washington D.C. We drove the Blue Ridge Parkway to the Smokey Mountains. We loved the scenery and are both into nature. We did have a bit of car trouble where the car just quit working but several really nice people came to help. The tow truck driver was extra helpful and stayed with us for two and a half hours while the car was fixed. After that we took off for Nashville Hall of Fame where we experienced the awesome Country Music, then we spent time in a bar listening to a lot of very talented singers who were hoping to be discovered. It was great. I loved it. We also shared a memorable chicken dinner before heading off to a cheap but pleasant hotel. Ken and I had such a great time. We are very happy together.

"Miracles are a retelling of the very same story,

which is written across the whole world in

letters too large

for some of us to see."

C.S. Lewis

Choroideremia

"In the right place at the right time."

My name is David Kay. I was born in 1944 in the Northwest Lake District town of Kendal, England also known as Kirbie Kendal, meaning "village with a church in the valley of the River Kent". Residents just call it Kendal. I was born with a challenge known as choroideremia, which is the inability to see well at night or in poor light. Individuals born with this rare x-linked recessive form of hereditary retinal degeneration experience a gradual loss of vision, starting with childhood night blindness, followed by peripheral vision loss, and progressing to loss of central vision later in life. Interestingly, choroideremia affects exclusively men. Female carriers have a 50%

chance of having either an affected son or a carrier daughter, while a male carrier will have all carrier daughters and unaffected sons. For this reason, my wife and I decided not to have children. And we wanted to travel and see the world.

I was told that at some point I would go totally blind. So it was no surprise that I had pretty good daytime vision and could drive until 1992 at which point I gave up my car. Ironically, the x-linked gene is carried only by females, and passed on only to males. My brother Peter, five years younger than me, never drove. His condition was a bit more serious than mine. He resides in Calgary, Canada. On the other hand, my brother John has not been affected at all.

I grew up in Kendal; my high school where I enjoyed a variety of sports was established in 1524. I received my degree in electrical engineering from the University of Salford in Manchester, England. Because of my major I was the first student apprentice employed by the War Office. My college fees were paid for. I believe in fate. Again, I was in the right place at the right time.

I was employed at the War Office, which was renamed after the war as The Ministry of Defense because I understood electronics and power lines and machines and drills. Later, an American company that had offices in Canada, Mexico, Trenton, Ontario and England employed me. The corporation employed about 15,000 people. In 1974, at age 29 I was given the opportunity to work in Shanghai, China for six weeks. The president of our office decided he could not be gone for such a long time so I ended up going with all these big executives. I was working in Erie, Pennsylvania for a company that manufactured electronic components and after working there for two years was representing the company in China. It happened like this (right place at the right time): I was standing in line at break time and the guy next to me starts chatting. He was the sales manager for our division and asked about my background. I told him electrical engineering and my last job was selling equipment. That got his attention. Next thing that happened is that he asked for my phone extension and he phoned me about an opening for sales engineer at another plant. The General Manager was British. "Are you interested? If so, we'll set you up." I got the job. I worked in Canada, all over the states, Shanghai for six weeks, also Taiwan, Hong Kong, and Tokyo.

By 1977 I'd been in Canada for five years. Our company was the only one to use the nearby Air Force base. We could jet from Erie across Lake Ontario. It was really cold in January in Ontario (opposite Rochester, NY). One evening, on a Friday night, snow came down horizontally. All you could see was the roof of my car. I came out, didn't have a power snow blower. I dug the car out. Went back into the house, took off my coat. I was sweaty. The phone rings, it's the sales manager in California asking me, "How would you like a job in California?" My answer: "What time did you want me to start?" I didn't even inquire about my new salary. My wife, Christine, and I moved to Orange County and bought a house in Tustin where we lived for 34 years. My new office was in Santa Ana. Later on, as my vision problems escalated, we decided to let go of our huge home with the pool and Jacuzzi, where it was a mile walk to the bus stop. There were no sidewalks in our neighborhood as it was an unincorporated area. Also, I was losing my vision.

After many years in our Tustin home we decided to move to Laguna Woods Village, where I had been selling electronic vision devices for several years. My wife could no longer drive, as she had developed a type of dementia. My side of the family is spread all over the globe. Christine's family members are all located in Northwest England: Yorkshire and Cumbria. So, after much consideration, we decided it would be best for her to live by her family, in a facility nearby where she would be cared for. Considering my visual challenges, I could no longer be her caregiver. One sad thing is that last September we would have celebrated our 50-year anniversary together. We've been apart for two years now.

I've lived in Laguna Woods for five years and use the Access bus to get around. I meet really interesting people in my business. Recently I met a woman who lives in Irvine, up in the Turtlerock area. Pamela, 87, is a retired United Air flight attendant who has developed macular degeneration. I fixed her Zoom Text machine and introduced her to my office assistant, Rachael, who has helped her out several times by driving her and just spending time with her.

I often consult with people to figure out the best technologies in vision devices for them. I set up the devices and train them how to use them. I do repair work on the machines and also around my own home. It takes me a bit longer to figure out things but I realize, in terms of vision, my hands are my eyes. When

I'm working with wiring I can't see colors. Once someone points out the colors, I can figure out what goes where and can use my handy screwdriver to fix things. If it's a plumbing problem, I just take things apart, clean them up, and put them back together again. I have a lot of confidence and a lot of patience. Once in a while, when it's taking me a long time to fix something, a few raunchy words seem to help. When I reach the cursing point it finally all comes together. Right place. Right time.

Recently I was recognized as an outstanding senior with Age Well Senior Services at the Florence Sylvester Senior Center for my help in assisting individuals like me who have compromised vision. I demonstrate screen reading and magnifying software. For the last 22 years I have been helping folks in Laguna Woods Village. I have worked with the Dayle McIntosh Center and the Braille Institute. I also installed the screen magnifier in the library at the Towers, an assisted living branch of Laguna Woods. Another thing I do is promote supplements for people with joint problems. I'm very active, love talking with people, and am looking forward to investigating LWV's Boomers Club.

As a youngster in Kendal, England, I played cricket, soccer, and rugby. I used to go out on long runs. I was pretty skinny at 17. A few years ago my weight got out of control and I found that I weighed about 252 pounds. We didn't eat junk food as kids but somehow it seemed to seep into my diet. In recent years I've been much more careful about eating. I'm back down to a healthy 180. I very much appreciate the Meals on Wheels program and all the volunteers who make the deliveries. I don't do much cooking. It's too scary using an electric stove but I'm pretty good at using my Microwave.

When some miracle cure comes along, I'll head down to Laguna Beach, stand near Las Brisas Restaurant, and once more look out at the ocean. That will truly be the right place at the right time.

"There are two ways to live: you can live as if nothing is a miracle; you can live as if everything is a miracle."

Albert Einstein

Doug's Story

People tell me that I inspire them, probably because of all that I have been through and the fact that I keep going. I'm six foot three inches tall. I was six feet in the ninth grade. I remember trick-or-treating with my school friends in sixth grade and having people say to me, "Don't you think you are too old to be out trick-or-treating?" I was in sixth grade! I was always tall for my age and active. I'm still physically active at 65 for having Parkinson's Disease.

I was raised from the age of 11 in Santa Ana, California. After graduating from Santa Ana High School in 1970, I enrolled at Cal State Long Beach. I completed my first semester and had an Atrio-Venus Malformation hemorrhage in my brain at the beginning of my second semester. I was getting ready for my retail job at Disneyland on a Saturday morning thank God. We only had one bathroom in our house, so my mom checked on me and found me in the bathtub in a coma. I was rushed to Santa Ana Community Hospital. That was February 27, 1971. I am an only child, so the doctor in charge revived me with the paddles and kept me alive for 24 minutes until I started breathing on my own again.

The stroke left me totally paralyzed on my left side, unable to move or talk. I had had a cerebral hemorrhage, a stroke, and was in a coma for five weeks in ICU. After two and a half months, when I regained consciousness, I was moved to UCI Medical Center in Orange for evaluation. My brain bleed was very deep in the center of the brain just above the thalamus. The thalamus is involved with motor and sensory functions, which is why I think I developed sudden onset Parkinson's.

Dr. Stanley Van Der Noort, who was head of Neurology at UCI Medical Center, was helping to evaluate me. He had heard of a 17-year old boy in Austria who had the same symptoms and was brought out of it by LevoDopa, the medication that is the Gold Standard for Parkinson's. I was basically non-functional, although I had gotten myself out of bed in the ward and started walking a little with the aid of a wheelchair.

When I started on LevoDopa it was very hard on my stomach. I had to eat something or take it with milk to soften the blow. Now it is buffered with CarbiDopa to settle the stomach. Originally I was taking six different medications a day, 24 pills in all.

So what kept me going? Originally a friend of mine from high school, Carol Stensrud, who was studying physical therapy, moved into our home to help me with keeping active. I had realized in the hospital that just because the physical therapy stopped, it didn't mean that it was not necessary anymore. We rode bikes, walked, exercised in our pool and I was back in charge of mowing a large sloping front yard with a push lawn mower.

Unfortunately, I ended up overdoing things, relapsed and was put back in the hospital for another month. After that my mother moved me into an apartment close to where she worked so she could check on me and make sure I was all right.

I was 19, had finished high school and had a semester at Cal State Long Beach under my belt. I wanted to go back to school, but one of the neurologists had told my mother not to waste her money because I only had half a brain left. So I decided to try a semester at Santa Ana Community College to see if I could still do the work. My friend told my teachers not to call on me or ask me questions because I couldn't speak loud enough to be heard. I had to carpool to school because I had lost my license due to the seizure I had experienced with the stroke.

I had a very successful semester at Santa Ana College and so I reapplied to Cal State Long Beach. I had decided to pursue a teaching career and enrolled as an English Composition and Linguistics major. I graduated in 1977 with my Bachelor of Arts Degree. To see if I would be compatible with teaching I took a job as a substitute teacher's aide with Santa Ana Unified. I loved working with the kids so I applied to the credential program at UC Irvine. I completed the work on my credential with student teaching first and fourth grades in Santa Ana Unified.

Carol, the high school friend who had helped me with physical therapy after my stroke, had gone on to get her Master's and was teaching at Chico State University in Chico, California. She recommended I consider moving to Chico because life was slower and less stressful in a small rural town. In 1980 I moved up to Chico. I then applied to the Masters Program in English at Chico State and was accepted.

Also, in Chico, to continue my commitment to ongoing physical therapy, I joined the Chico Sports Club and soon found myself engaged in Nancy Weigman's yoga class. I really took to yoga very seriously because it was helping me a great deal. It not only aids in muscle strength and stretching, it also helps with breathing and meditative relaxation, all of which helps with the effects of Parkinson's Disease. I have done yoga ever since and swear it is what keeps me going!

Through the 1980's I worked on my Masters degree. I finally graduated in 1989. I concentrated my studies in English Second Language. During my last couple of years as a student I worked with the tutorial program for ESL students at the university and eventually took over as the leader of the program. I wrote my Masters Thesis on "The Differences in Learning Styles between Arab and Asian Post Secondary Students". In 1990 I was hired as an ESL teacher by the University English Department, which oversaw the ESL program. That was a great thrill for me as I felt that all my work had finally been recognized. When I started teaching, the program consisted of mostly Arab students. They were interesting and a pleasure to work with. We actually had a Saudi Prince in our program.

I lived in Chico for 30 years with my partner whom I met there. We had a great life together traveling a good deal around the globe. We toured southern Europe, Australia, and spent two weeks in Puerta Vallarta every year for ten years with friends. Unfortunately, as my Parkinson's progressed we started to grow apart and we parted ways, but on good terms.

In 2010 I moved back down to Southern California to live with my mother, Pearl Berry, in Laguna Woods. My mom is now 91 years old and is still very active. She still drives very well and invests in the stock market. She worked many years for a stock brokerage in Santa Ana. She inspires me! Laguna Woods is a wonderful retirement community. There are more than 200 clubs here for every kind of interest and hobby you can imagine. Also, Saddleback Community College offers 75 classes in our community. There are art, learning and physical education courses to avail yourself of right here. I always say, "If you live here and you are bored, it's your own fault."

I have been the Recording Secretary of the Dog Club for six years and was President of the Rainbow Club, the Village LGBT club, for three years. The Rainbow Club is a great support organization for LGBT residents of Laguna Woods.

In the meantime, my Parkinson's symptoms continue to increase slowly, thank goodness. I have a motto that I live by: "Use it or lose it." So I just keep going no matter what. If I have a particular pain or problem, I find a way to work around it to keep moving. At 52 I got my first dog from a breeder, a Westie I named Bonnie. I realized she was walking funny so I took her to the Vet. It turned out she had a dislocated patella, a slipping knee cap. But she always insisted on taking long walks and the problem would be better the more she walked. It finally completely went away after a few years. I have walked up to five miles a day with my dogs Bonnie and Fiona. Sadly, I lost Bonnie this last year, but Fiona and I continue to walk long walks. Bonnie inspired me; in that even though you have a problem, try to work it out. It is so important to keep physically active and engaged no matter what difficulty you experience in life. I've always belonged to a gym and you know what I have noticed? On January 1st the gym is full, but by February it's down to about half-full. People have the right intentions. They just don't follow through. I knew that after my physical therapy in the hospital was finished, it didn't just stop there. That is why I have always maintained a gym membership. I'm still in physical therapy, just self-directed. Also, my gym membership in Chico led me to start yoga. I have continued to practice yoga for about 25 years now. I swear it is one of the main activities that keeps me going strong. I can often stop my Parkinson's tremors with yoga breathing and meditation.

Yoga tones and strengthens the muscles and keeps me flexible. It is a great life practice! As my body struggles a bit more, I meditate, keep focused on "now" and to look inside myself for answers to physical problems. I keep focused on the positive aspects of life. Negativity is so unhealthy. So, maintain a positive attitude towards life. Stay physically and mentally active. And don't focus on the past. It's over! Focus on the future!

"I think miracles exist in part as gifts and in part as clues that there is something beyond the flat world we see."

Peggy Noonan

Eric

My name is Eric Rasmussen. I was born in 1944 in the City of Orange, Orange County, California. I grew up in the golden days of the citrus growing regions of Orange County where orange groves spanned for miles and miles, and as children we were free to ride our bicycles up and down the two-lane roads that crisscrossed the area.

As a small child I was active, always climbing a tree or a trellis, digging in the dirt as deep as I could and learning a love of woodworking that has been a joy throughout my life. As a youngster I was a good student, maybe a bit of a renegade, but as a boy it wasn't always easy sitting still in a classroom. When I was ten years old, my thirteen-year old brother died in a drowning accident, in a neighbor's swimming pool. That event changed my life.

I went on to please my parents by being an excellent student. Graduated from Orange High School in 1962, moved to Berkeley, California to attend the University of California to start my freshman year. Completing my Bachelor Degree in Business Administration in 1966, I continued on to excel and complete my MBA at Berkeley in 1968. After applying my MBA in the printing industry for a few years, I was unfulfilled and decided I really wanted to become a professor of English Literature. I applied to and was accepted at San Francisco State University where I completed my Masters of English Literature in 1971. I then discovered, much to my dismay, that a professor at the university level made less money than bus drivers for the San Francisco Transit.

So, realizing that I had learned to think critically, write expressively and read comprehensively, I decided to become a lawyer! I enrolled in Golden Gate University at the age of 30 and graduated in 1978, passing the California Bar Exam on my first try. My career as a lawyer, specializing in Business, Real Estate, and Estate planning spanned the years of 1978 until my recent retirement in 2012.

In early 2007 I started experiencing difficulty eating, getting a fork from the plate to my mouth. My face was exhibiting mask-like expressions. My balance was noticeably impaired and my motor skills movements were slowing. It was almost like I'd had some small strokes. I was terrified. After doing my own extensive research on my current symptoms, I then consulted my General Practice Doctor who referred me to a neurologist. I was originally seen by one neurologist, didn't care for his "bedside manner" so I pursued and discovered one of the most highly acclaimed neurologists here in Orange County and have been under his excellent care for the past nine years. I was diagnosed with Parkinson's. I knew I had some disease before that. In fact I later found out that people asked why I always looked at my feet when walking. I believe that I may have been exposed to toxic chemicals when I was young. Because I grew up among the orange groves of Orange, and because these trees were sprayed with chemicals, I feel certain that contributed to the Parkinson's that seems to have affected so many people. This was the pesticide spray that was routinely sprayed on the orange groves in the 1950's. Thanks to Rachael Carson's book Silent Spring where she questioned the logic of broadcasting potentially dangerous chemicals into the environment with little investigation into the impact on health effects on humans and wildlife, DDT was finally banned in 1972, ten years after her book was published.

The other theory that I am working on is heavy metals. I believe that this may also be a factor. I'm still researching that possible cause. As a precautionary measure, I recently had all of the metal fillings in my teeth replaced. And somewhere in my searching for answers, I found that keeping a bar of soap under my sheets at night stopped my leg tremors. I even keep a bar of soap in my pocket during the day. I'm not sure why this works. Maybe it's the placebo effect, but for me, it's been an amazing discovery that I'm eager to share with others. To keep myself in shape and to stay as healthy as possible for as long as possible, I exercise four or five days a week. My physical therapist, Claire McLean, specializes in exercises for a Parkinson's group. She coaches me and keeps me moving. Twice a week I meet with a private trainer and in addition I attend a yoga class when I can. I used to box, which kept me moving my arms and legs but that has become difficult so I now practice yoga at the yoga studio in Orange. It's called SunSpark.

My wife, Yvonne, and I now live in my family home where I grew up. About 18 years ago, we moved in, and over the years have made many updates, renovations, and improvements. We are grateful to have three-fourths of an acre of fruit trees, gardens, outbuildings, and a beautiful backyard resort featuring a heated swimming pool, where we often do water exercises.

For many years we have attended church on Sunday mornings. We've been involved in a small support group of about 20 people and I'm grateful that they pray for me and with me. We've formed strong friendships and I feel emotionally supported. Understanding that Parkinson's is a progressive disease, Yvonne and I endeavor to travel and adventure all that we can, while I am still highly mobile. With that in mind, we feel very fortunate to be able to travel often.

We recently celebrated our 30th wedding anniversary with the better part of a month in Europe exploring Barcelona, Spain, Cote d' Azur, France, Rome, and the wine regions of Umbria and Tuscany. Our travel itineraries always take into consideration the accommodations for my need to sometimes rest. In the Fall, we usually spend two weeks in Maui.

In February a ten-day cruise to the Caribbean out of Tampa, Florida had us visiting the parts of Key West, Florida, the Grand Turks on the Island of Turks, Caicos, the Bahamas, and the Dominican Republic. After the cruise we spent four days in Florida with friends. In springtime this year we joined friends in Cancun, Mexico for a week of sun, fun, and eating. In November we'll spend 15 days cruising from San Pedro, California to the Hawaiian Islands including nine days at sea.

There is an annual Parkinson's retreat in Scottsdale, Arizona hosted by the world renowned PWR Gym in Tucson. PWR stands for Parkinson Wellness Recovery. I get four hours a day of therapy. My wife and other supporters of Parkinson's attend lectures by renowned neurologists. I really feel like being as physical as possible is very beneficial for me. As they say "exercise is medicine."

One of the speakers at this retreat will be Dr. Frank C. Church. He was diagnosed with Parkinson's in 2004. He offers the following reassuring theme for anyone with Parkinson's: "I am still here, and you're still here. We both have a lot yet to offer. Stay strong, stay hopeful, and stay you." With or without Parkinson's, Frank's message will empower you to "live decisively in the forward direction. Stay focused, and be persistent. Please. Don't give up."

"Miracles, in the sense of phenomena we cannot explain, surround us on every hand; life itself is the miracle of miracles."
George Bernard Shaw

Growing Up As a Cleft Palate Child

Jack L. Housden, BS, MED, EDD

Seventy-six years ago I was born into the body of a human being that was flawed by a common, world-wide birth defect named cleft palate. Cleft palate is an anomaly where the fetus fails to fuse completely the mandible, upper lip, nostrils, and the palate, thereby leaving a gap in those regions of the face. The baby cannot suckle in the normal manner, due to the inability of the mouth to create a tight seal to create a vacuum.

Upon reflection, I am struck by how shocked my parents must have been to gaze upon their second-born child and see this helpless, grotesque-looking baby looking back at them. What a jolt that must have been in their lives. Whatever they experienced, it was never, ever talked about or shared with me. In their eyes I was no different than anybody else's child, except for necessary surgical repairs to my cleft palate, which were smoothly integrated into our daily lives, as I grew.

My first memory, when I was two, was being on the Greyhound Bus in Brewster, Washington with my mother traveling to the Children's Orthopedic Hospital in Seattle, Washington, which was for the first surgical repair of my cleft palate. The surgeons were sufficiently skilled in 1943 to surgically fuse my mandible, upper lip, nose and palate so that as my body grew those parts of my anatomy could grow naturally in tandem. The Children's Orthopedic Hospital did this free of charge. To this day, my favorite charity is Smile Train, the non-profit organization that does cleft palate repair surgeries around the world.

Our family, as was true for so many during and after WWII, scraped and scratched out a living with my father employed as a farm laborer and my mother being a homemaker who could do virtually everything it took to keep a family in food, clothing, and shelter. Every autumn during harvest, there would be weeks of canning of green beans, tomatoes, peaches, and other food items. My Dad would slaughter hogs, butcher a heifer, and shoot a deer, cut the meat into meal-sized packets and take them to the rented freezer-locker in town, which was five miles away. My mother raised chickens for the eggs and the meat. My dad and mom both milked the cow, depending upon who could spare the time. The important message here is that I lived a simple life growing up from age six to age 12. During that time our family grew to include four children. My parents were so preoccupied with providing food, clothing, and shelter for the family that they had very little time or energy to give to their kids. This was a good thing for me, because I was expected to take care of myself; to be responsible for looking out for

50

my own safety; to entertain myself; and to decide for myself what I wanted to do when I wanted to do it.

As I began school in first grade at Brewster Elementary School, in Brewster, Washington, I had the same first grade teacher, Mrs. Moore, and the same second grade teacher, Mrs. Emerson, as my older brother, my mother, and my father. I never felt that I was treated differently than my classmates, but I knew I looked different because of my harelip and because of my marginally intelligible, rapid, nasal speech. I was acutely aware of being stared at by curious kids. When asked by other kids "what's wrong with you?" I would answer, "I can't help it. I was born that way." Fortunately, I was an above average learner. I could hit and throw a baseball with accuracy. I could run as fast as most of my classmates. What I couldn't do was to play a wind instrument in music class, because I couldn't close off my soft palate to create a seal that would permit me to blow up a balloon, suck through a straw, whistle a tune, or blow with enough force to play a wind instrument. So, I simply didn't do those things. In first grade I gradually moved from group three to group two and up to group one in oral reading, which was a triumph for me knowing that my speech was difficult to understand. But that didn't seem to matter with my classmates. Jack was simply a fun-loving, cheerful friend to every one of them. I had no desire to compete, to be the best, or to excel in anything in school. My parents rarely, if ever, said anything, one way or the other, about my school report card. They just signed it and gave it to me to take back to the teacher. I was expected to do my best. That is all that was ever asked of me.

Then, at age 12 and continuing on as I graduated high school and college, things began to happen. My Dad landed a job with the State of Oregon with the Department of Fish and Game as a gamekeeper on a State Game Farm. Our family of six, including four children, moved five miles out of the town of

Hermiston, Oregon. I entered sixth grade at Westside Elementary School in Hermiston as a transfer from Brewster Elementary School. I quickly assimilated into my new classroom, easily making new friends, and excelling in my schoolwork. I instantly went from being a C student in my previous school to being an A student in my new school.

Oh, those teen age years. As I entered junior high school, I was very self-conscious of my appearance. I felt unattractive because of my harelip and my hard-to-understand speech. My lip and nose had been "surgically adjusted" by surgeons at the University of Oregon Medical School in Portland as my adult facial features developed. (These cosmetic and functional cleft palate surgeries were also provided free of charge.) I was provided speech correction therapy at Eastern Oregon College in La Grande, Oregon, which helped a little. However, these cleft palate accommodations had an adverse affect on my self-image, because they drew attention to the fact that I was "different," which is not how I saw myself. I tended to withdraw from social contact and became purposefully non-verbal in classroom interactions. Occasionally teachers would call on me to answer a question no one else could answer or to ask for my point of view on the topic. I always knew the answers and I always expressed my opinions. My grades were mostly A's with a once in a while B. I was an excellent student and highly respected by my classroom peers. One day the school counselor pulled me out of class and sat me down in a room by myself and asked me to take this test. It was an IQ test. She told me that she was right, that the information in my student file was not accurate.

In retrospect, although I secretly harbored these feelings of not being worthy, my classmates voted me class president, captain of our intramural team, and as a student representative to the student council. I wasn't "popular," but I was well-regarded by my peers. I even had a girlfriend, bless her loving heart. Lela Johnson, aka, Lela Keim now. She has remained a treasured friend to this day.

During my first year in high school, my mother fell in love with another man and left our traditional nuclear family in pursuit of her happiness. She eloped with her lover taking with her my younger brother and sister, leaving my older brother, Bob, and me in the care of our dad. This was my first big lesson in forgiveness. Although I briefly grieved the loss of my dear Mother from my daily life, I latched on to the truth that her happiness was what mattered. I quickly forgave my mother for all transgressions of social conventions that affected anyone else, including me. It was a heartbreaking experience, but a great lesson that I have carried throughout my lifetime.

Shortly after our nuclear family breakup, something else happened. My brother Bob and I were driving to school on February 6, 1957, and we had a wreck. My physical body was severely traumatized by the crash. I nearly died. I was in a coma for a week due to kidney failure, and again learned a valuable lesson about life. Expect a miracle. My kidneys came back to life, and the rest of my body had to play catch-up. I was on the critical condition list with 24-hour nursing care for five weeks. It truly was one of the most difficult experiences of my life. I had a brush with death and I lived!

Another lesson learned – GRATITUDE. I am grateful for this life I have been given, and this cleft palate thing is just a minor distraction, nothing more. In high school I made an agreement with myself. I was never going to take school homework home. I got my homework done in class, at a study hall, during lunch break, on the bus riding home, and at other opportune moments. School was school and everything else was there for fun. I loved playing ball, fishing, hunting, hiking, and shooting hoops in my backyard. So, I took easy classes instead of the ones that the college-bound kids took. I had no concept, no idea of what I was going to do after high school. I didn't give it a thought. Which brings me to another moment of the expect-a-miracle lesson. After completing my junior year, during the summer one Sunday afternoon, I was hocking watermelons along the roadside in a rural region of Hermiston, Oregon, along with my friend Dennis Schultz, and a guy stopped by to buy a watermelon. We talked about the weather, the watermelons, and other stuff and then he asked me a question I was not prepared for.

He asked: "What are you going to do after you graduate from high school?"

I replied truthfully, "I don't know."

He handed me his card, telling me he was a vocational rehabilitation counselor with the State of Oregon, and he said that if I wanted to go to college maybe he could help me pay for it at one of our Oregon colleges. I perked up. Money to go to college? No way I could afford to go to college. I didn't have any money. I told him that I was interested and that going to college sounded like fun. He took my name and school information and said he would be by this fall to see what we could work out. I forgot all about it until early in October of my senior year the intercom crackled in my classroom and spoke.

"Is Jack Housden in there?"

The teacher replied back "Yes, he is."

"Send him to the office please," came back the reply.

I can still feel that jolt of fear that went through me. "What have I done now?" Long story made short: it was the vocational rehabilitation counselor fulfilling his promise. I chose to apply to Oregon State University because they had the best athletic programs. The school counselors transferred me out of my advance metal shop, study hall, and creative art classes and into advanced algebra, trigonometry, and college prep English classes. Voc Rehab would pay for my tuition and books and room and board. All I had to do was to show up and keep from flunking out. That was a good deal.

After graduating high school, I showed up at Oregon State University and began my classes, living in an old dormitory. I had a lot of fun. Nobody paid any attention to my harelip or my speech defect. My first year I was a geology major and earned a 3.13 GPA as a freshman, which thoroughly surprised my rehab counselor. I changed majors as a junior to mathematics, falsely believing that with a career in computer programming and computer technology, I could just blend into the woodwork of life and not have to compete with non-cleft palate, speech handicapped individuals. Fortunately, my rehab counselor suggested that I get a prosthetic palate appliance that would correct my speech into the normal range of voice and diction, thereby giving me more options of career choices. Vocational Rehabilitation in the State of Oregon paid the costs of creating this device, which worked perfectly. I graduated from OSU with a Bachelor's degree and without a speech impediment. Here was another example of expect-a-miracle.

I will admit that this cleft palate thing created a lot of stuff in my childhood that needed to be healed as I was growing in intimate relationship maturity, in career choices, in my aspirations, and in my spiritual development during my 20's, 30's, 40's, and 50's. I have just kept on doing my best at whatever I was involved in. I opened this brief essay with the idea that "I was born into this body of a human being." I am one of the fortunate individuals who was introduced to the belief that I am not my body and I am not my mind. I am a soul traveling though the Universe taking a journey on Planet Earth in a human body. I have personally experienced being physically out of my body hovering above, looking down at my body, considering it and making the choice to return to it. I believe that all of what has shown up in my life is of my own making and that I was all that time being prepared to be a loving partner for my soul mate, Kathie.

"The miracle is this: the more we share, the more we have." Leonard Nimoy

Joyce Noh

Having been blind from birth, I have always been fascinated and curious about the sounds I hear from the surrounding environment. This curiosity led me to get interested in various musical instruments, but my actual journey as a pianist started when I turned thirteen years old and moved to the United States from South Korea. The late start and overcoming cultural barriers as an immigrant created various hardships in advancing my journey.

However, the fulfillment I found in expressing music by delivering my heart and soul to my fingertips motivated me to press on and continue my musical education at the New England Conservatory of Music. By furthering my music through the Doctor of Musical Arts in Performance (DMA) program, I not only desire to inspire and challenge other disabled artists and audiences around the world, but also to disciple and cultivate a new generation of blind musicians.

As a blind person, I know that people with disabilities need not only a lot of resources, but also a role model to follow. Particularly, I dream to perform for the disabled people around the world, so that I can inspire and challenge them, to see if they have the heart and determination to do something, they can overcome their disability. Moreover, I hope to make disciples of younger blind generations by discovering their musical talent and helping them to maximize their potentials.

Some might say that I am an idealist but this is what I precisely yearn to do: to both motivate and cultivate. I desire to refine myself as an inspirational concert pianist and a motivational mentor.

"If we could see the miracle of a single flower clearly, our whole life would change."

Buddha

My Story with MS

Marilyn Stark

"Do you want to take a shot once a week or every other day?"

When I picked my jaw up off the floor, I asked: "Do I have diabetes?"

"No, you have MS.

"What's MS? I don't understand."

This conversation took place in the doctor's office in 1995. I had back pain so my general doctor had sent me to a specialist. I knew nothing of MS or its effects or symptoms. After a spinal tap to confirm the doctor's proclamation, I now had a decision to make. I told only my parents and a few other people at church. One of my church friends was a lady in a wheelchair with MS. She and I talked and talked.

I did not tell anyone at school where I taught. I did not tell my friends. I wasn't embarrassed, but felt I needed to keep it to myself. I had burning back pain and buzzing or tingling in my arms and hands and could not step up or down a curb or stair without holding on to something; at least with my fingertips.

In 1995, I made a trip to Russia, Austria, England, and New York. I did take a fold-up cane with me but most thought it was a fashion statement. In 1997, I went to Kenya; again no one knew the truth and my fashion statement went with me. I met the President of Kenya and made the front page of the paper. I met the King of Five-Bush Tribe. His badge of office was to wear an electric blue suit from the 1950's. He had to speak five languages as each tribe had its own dialect.

In the classroom, I walked around but made sure I had something to touch for balance. Walking across campus was a trick so I found I walked the long way around so the wall was within fingertip closeness. But, still no one knew. I sometimes used a staff and the school thought I was just that crazy old teacher showing off again.

I was in my classroom in the fall of 2000. Walking around my class I had tables to touch. I heard an audible snap as if someone had snapped his or her fingers. At once I knew my back was no longer on fire and my arms and hands no longer tingled. If this is true, maybe my knees worked, so I started jumping up and down. My students thought nothing of this, as they already knew I was crazy.

As soon as I arrived home, I called my mother in Illinois. The first thing she said was, "Are you missing something?" I asked, "How did you know?" She replied, "I was raking the leaves and praying for you and a voice said:

"It is done!"

I stopped using a staff and walked without touching anything. I went to the doctor and surprise, surprise. I no longer had the MS symptoms or effects.

In 2001, I retired from teaching after 29 years. On the last day I told my principal about the MS. She didn't believe me but just smiled. In June of 2001, I left my home in the capable hands of my son and three other young men. Was this a mistake? I guessed I'd find out later.

The drive from California to Illinois took four days. My parents insisted I not drive alone. So, after asking everyone I knew, the only person with time to travel was the son of a fellow church member. I had never met this young man nor knew anything about him.

Four-thirty a.m. is a rude awakening for anyone. The young man was not ready to leave. With no real preparation or supplies (luggage) we left California for Illinois.

As soon as he got in the car, he said, "My mother said you are very smart. Teach me everything you know."

So I started at the beginning. Genesis 1:1. In the beginning God . . . I soon learned why he had time to travel. He had just gotten out of jail and had no job. The young man was dropped off at the airport in St. Louis late at night and flew home. I drove on to Illinois and got to Decatur at 2:00 a.m.

I was hired to teach algebra for the 2001-2002 school year at a local high school, but I had gone to Illinois to help my parents. My Father was 98 and my Mother 95. Mother was in good health but my Father passed away in December 2001. I had tickets to go to Israel and Egypt in the fall of 2001. Unfortunately, 9/11 occurred and my Father said, "You can't leave the country." I did not go, but had travel insurance and recovered my money.

I began teaching special education instead of math and did that for the next ten years. However, in 2003 I did go to Egypt and had the adventure of a lifetime. I took my folding cane with me but seldom unfolded it. Mother and I traveled by car to New York, Florida, Louisiana, California and back to Illinois. This took about two and a half months. Mother's health was very good. So was mine.

I went to England in 2004 with my sister-in-law and came home on the QE II. Watching TV one day, I saw a sports event called the Triathlon. I said to myself if ever there was a sport I wanted to do, that was it. An armchair athlete like me seldom actually does any more than watch. In 2007, I got the chance to knock off one more bucket list item. I did two triathlons in one year. The YMCA held the event in a very special way. A triathlon is swimming 2-1/2 miles, biking 112 miles and running a marathon of 26.2 miles.

The YMCA set it up. You use the pool and equipment and record your time and have six weeks to finish the course. My first triathlon took 18 hours and my second took only 9 hours. I got a t-shirt for my effort.

Along with this exercise, I was teaching doing AWANAs (a children's program), teaching senior algebra, teaching a Bible study, teaching a Jr. High Sunday school class and running sound in church. Mother had many activities so I needed to drive her most days.

2011 finds me with tickets to go to England for a special walking tour. Fourth of July weekend 2011. A Friday at about 5:00 p.m. I felt as if someone sucker-punched me in the gut and I was in pain and had a fever and it was rising. Mom tried to help with soup and jello but by Saturday evening I was delirious. The neighbor called 911 and I had surgery for a ruptured appendix, which had gone into peritonitis. This had me in the hospital for two weeks.

By this time, Mom is now 105 but still knitting a blanket about every two weeks, going to Bible study, church, shopping and visiting her few friends still with us on planet earth. We liked to take long drives around Illinois and see places we would hear about.

Two weeks after I got out of the hospital, at the beginning of August, the doctor suggested I get a blood test to check for any leftover peritonitis from the appendix. The results showed I now had cancer –multi-myeloma. This means my blood makes a protein I shouldn't have and my blood eats holes in my bones. I've seen the pictures and my bones from head to toe look like Swiss cheese. Some holes are tiny but others aren't. Chemo is started. I don't lose my hair, thank goodness. I go in and sit for two to four hours for the drip, drip, drip of the fluid into my hand. Finding a vein often meant I went home with three or four Band-Aids per hand.

Remember that England walking tour? So long to England, but I had insurance and got my money back. Remember mom? Well the end of October she is doing very well. The 105 year-old, knitting every day, shopping, church, friends, very active, has a stroke after a day of going to a tea party and shopping. She loses her left side and can't swallow. Her mind is still clear and she can talk. She remembers her students, who they married, how many children they have and what kind of work they do. She keeps up to date with all the people who come to visit and share gossip. I go each day to help her do her exercises.

Second week of November, I can't work my right foot so I have to stop driving a car. Friends squire me around to see mom, buy food and get to church. I am not teaching, as of September due to my chemo. By Thanksgiving Day, my brother and family drive from New York State and find me in a chair I can't get out of. Day after Thanksgiving, I move to a senior care home. The home is across the street from our house. My room is facing the road so I could watch the house every day.

On Monday, I go to my cancer doctor to find out why I can't walk. My oncologist sends me to a neurologist who takes one look at me and puts me in the hospital without even time for me to go home. The neurologist says, "You have one of two things – one will kill you and the other will not."

I later learn he didn't think I would make it through the night. Geon Berra means I get a shunt in my neck and spend two hours a day in dialysis. My blood is drained out, the platelets removed and then new platelets from someone else are put back into my blood and I get my blood back. Five weeks I spend in the hospital. Meanwhile, my Mom hasn't seen me. She gives up.

I go back to the nursing home the day before Christmas. On January 8th, Mom dies. I end up back in the hospital taking dialysis again.

After three weeks the doctor says, "You aren't getting better so I'm going to do a spinal tap."

After the second spinal tap where they couldn't get any fluid, they decide I have MS. Here we go again. The doctor wants me to take shots every other day. But, the medicine has so many side effects. It is worse than the disease. I find my own method. I start with naplia. It really worked. By July, I return to California and start a whole new adventure.

Facts as of July 2012:

#1.   I can't walk so I'm using a wheelchair.

#2.   I have to reclaim my house.

Remember my son and the three guys —
surprise-- they did a good job in the eleven
years. Everything worked and the house was
A-OK!

Getting back in the swing, I found I
wanted to teach so I started teaching Adult
Education. I'm still at it, teaching ESL to
wonderful "kids." I still swim twice a week. In
my spare time I write, read, and paint. On one
day a week I shop and then push myself home
– downhill.

In 2016 I did a zipline and can't wait to
do it again. Travel is not in my future as of this
writing but when I can, I will.

"I am realistic. I expect miracles."

Wayne Dyer

Richard's Story

In 1967 my body went through several brief but curious episodes that would soon lead to a diagnosis of a disease I knew nothing about, a disorder that had the potential to haunt the remainder of my life. For the next fifty years I was to experience random disruptions of physical abilities that most accomplish without a second thought. My right leg would refuse to follow the commands it received, requiring special attention, even then inefficiently proceeding. Or my left hand would begin to loose sensitivity, touching and grasping no longer accomplished with regularity. Second, third and fourth thoughts became necessary to overcome these short-circuited Central Nervous System (CNS) commands. But even then, success was far from guaranteed. Abnormal sensitivities would become benchmarks of my daily life.

My balance and strength was to become challenged with each passing year, wearing away layers of the Self that I knew as Richard.

How could I possibly have known that this was my destiny? I was 18 years old, a senior in high school, on my way to UC Irvine. My future was promising; my today was shining. How could I have imagined what the Universe had in store for me on that day in 1967, when, after weeks of tests, the physician said, "I'm sorry, Mrs. Snyder, but I think your boy has Multiple Sclerosis."

MS didn't come right out and smack me hard. No, each episode, or EXACERBATION, began gradually: deterioration heightening, peaking, then fading, leaving little evidence of its visit. Legs, arms and hands were the usual targets but speech and vision troubles were included. From start to finish, exacerbations lasted an average of 6-8 weeks, never affecting multiple areas simultaneously.

For the first 15-20 years of my post-1967 life, the progression of my body's MS was slow but steady. I'd notice an exacerbation creeping in, an area losing receptivity, wait for it to play-out, then enjoy my near-normality until the next invasion neared. About twice a year I could expect an exacerbation and throughout those years, targets of attack were hit multiple times. This phase, designated RELAPSING/REMITTING, is the most common beginning for those with MS, occurring in about 85% of patients.

Because so little was known about MS in the late 60's, drug therapies were in their infancy. My early exacerbations were treated with PREDNISONE, a steroid that was thought to lower the intensity and shorten the duration. Maybe it did, hard to say. But I soon learned of a researcher at the University of Oregon in Portland with a holistic approach that I became confident would benefit me, as well as causing less BIG PHARMA HARM to my body; I began following The Swank Diet.

While scientific data can't confirm Dr. Roy Swank's "treatment", anecdotal accounts from the hundreds of patients worldwide who followed the Swank Protocol will vouch for its success. I am confident my experiences reflect the benefits I gained by following Dr. Roy's ideas. And because I so often felt this diet was all I needed, I didn't ever begin any of the "new" MS therapies that were being developed.

Since the early 1990's, my body has been on the gradual but steady decline path referred to as SECONDARY PROGRESSIVE MS. At some point, the exacerbations ceased, replaced by balance, strength and endurance issues, all functions and effects of each other. For the last thirty years this gradual ebb has been buffered by my refusal to give-in. As I approach my body's 50-year anniversary of being sentenced to the complications of MS, I can truthfully say that "suffering from MS" was never an option in my life. Outside of the two curious diagnosis-confirming symptoms in 1967, what my body has experienced has been predictable; there have been no abrupt shifts, no sudden, dramatic shocks, no awaking to find my leg unresponsive. The creeping-up of effects gave me opportunity for daily assessments, chances to make adaptations as needed. I generally knew what to expect and how long I'd need to endure and adjust. The only pain that was presented by my body's MS came from mishaps: falls, abrasions, cracked ribs, and broken bones-usually resulting from over-compensations in my 24/7 adaptations as I was maintaining awareness of the surroundings.

And I sure have accomplished a bunch and had fun doing it! From 1972 to 2001 I taught young Einsteins in the Westminster Elementary School District, impacting some 3,000 kids, from 2nd through 8th grades. Yeah, there were a few Bozos mixed in but, for the most part, each day was a new, enlivening experience. Most of my competitive sports days are history but I'm still able to exercise in the pool. I've been on four or five cruises, toured France, England, Ireland, Italy, Scotland both in group settings and with just my Lover. We've taken numerous road trips, enjoying more than half of our Fifty, Nifty, United States. There have been lots of Mexico trips, as well as Alaska and Hawaii adventures. In most of these cases, my electric Rascal scooter was my best friend. ADA regulations make it easy for us differently-abled travelers to experience all we will allow ourselves to do. Why, tomorrow my Sensational Sue will be waving good-bye as I fly from Santa Ana to Reno-Tahoe for a four night, on-my-own, resort adventure. While my body challenges me, I can't let it keep me down.

Partially because MS didn't suddenly slam my body like so many other physical heartbreaks, I've never (99% never) gotten comfort from adding the, "Why did this have to happen to me?" mantra to my 'Story Inventory'. Nor are "Poor me", "I'm so unlucky", and, "It's not Fair!" among my rants. Of course it's not fair. Life has NO fair guarantees, no justice warranties, no do-overs for unfortunate outcomes. Life Just Is! It's how one plays the cards they were dealt that makes or breaks the goodness life has to offer.

You've probably noticed the several times I've repeated the thought "It's my body that has MS." At some point I realized I'm so much more than my physical body and I refuse to give in to the thought that "I have MS." I Don't Have MS! The *I Am* is too powerful a concept to allow any negative ideas to penetrate it. And what about The Soul that chose to be me? Yes, I do believe we have spirits that have incarnated, an energy that guides our lives, spirits that have been here before, souls that have lessons to learn, lessons to teach. Could that be the *I Am* that has guided me to the knowing that life can be so much more than the circumstances I encounter?

Another healing discovery I've made was to realize just how powerful my thoughts are! How much space do I want to give to negative ideas? Do I want to be right or do I want to be happy? Can I live in Principle or do I want to let Circumstances direct my thoughts? I'm the one responsible for my happiness. Things happen. How they affect me is up to me. Life is Cause-Effect driven. Every event has the power to affect me in any number of ways. Can I take what many might see as painful and not allow the pain to overwhelm me? Can I let the past be the past, the future to be worry-free? The more I'm able to live in The Today, the greater the comfort I'll achieve.

If I'm looking for someone out there who'll make me happy, I'm doomed to failure. Happiness is an 'Inside Job'. Finding my Soul Mate, my Sensational Sue, was a direct result of seeking another already internally complete; neither of us needed someone to make us happy. What we each found was a partner with whom we could share and build individual joy. I've come to the conclusion that the purpose of Life is to give and receive Love.

As my life has progressed it has become easier to ask for and receive help: rising from a chair, climbing a stair, retrieving a dropped item, accessing my electric scooter from the van. People observe and often offer help. By responding graciously I not only decrease my risks, I validate their need to give. Even when I don't need a hand, I'm always sure to thank and encourage their efforts. "Don't stop asking, even if your intentions are rebuffed; accepted or not, the Love you offer is what's important." The more stress I can eliminate, the less likely I am going to falter.

The one prescriptive drug I've incorporated into my life is Modafinil, marketed by Cephalon as Provigil. Prescribed off-label for MS, it's a sleep-inhibitor that allows me to remain alert and stronger longer. Its effects are similar to (in my mind) caffeine, which stimulates brain activity by blocking neurons from absorbing calming molecules; Provigil works by...well, they don't really know how or why it works; it just does.

In this journey I get the opportunity to make lots of choices. I've chosen NOT to 'suffer' from MS, not to be a 'victim'. I've chosen therapies that others warned were ineffective. When faced with daunting situations, I've chosen to see many of them as opportunities. Change your thinking, Change your life has become my mantra. What I've done has worked for me.

When someone asks my Sensational Sue, "How long has he been handicapped?", she whispers, "Shsshh...he doesn't know he's handicapped. Don't tell him."

As with most Thinkers, we seem to find ourselves questioning, "Why am I here? What's my purpose for being alive?"

Besides the basic Universal Purpose – "Be givers and takers of Love", I've decided my job is to share my disability. How can I help others to see the truth of their situation, to see they have so much to offer by living their life to the fullest, maintaining and expanding their feeling of empowerment?

Until I no longer can, should that day sneak up on me, I'll continue to press on, acknowledging the presence of MS in my body, but never letting it dominate. I'll continue to be a Love Magnet, absorbing and reflecting the joy that comes my way, knowing the annoyance that's MS cannot stop me.

"Seeing, hearing and feeling are miracles, and each part and tag of me is a miracle."

Walt Whitman

Sam's Story

My first experience with MS was a complete surprise. While sitting in my car in San Diego at work, my entire left side went numb. I knew something was wrong. Suddenly the numbness left but at that point, it seems like damage had been done. The next day I was off to Kaiser Hospital where a diagnosis of MS was made. I was 59 years old. Now I'm 76.

Let's not forget Pauline. She's my special girlfriend who keeps reminding me to stay positive. We live in Laguna Woods Village with lots of retired folks. Almost daily we go over to a little park on the corner to sit in the sun and read our books. I don't walk very well so I get around in my electric scooter.

We've just returned from Mexican Riviera cruise. It was a blast. My advice? Don't cave in to self-pity. Keep going.

"Miracles happen everyday, change your perception of what a miracle is and you'll see them all around you."

Jon Bon Jovi

Michael Smuland

It was April of 1982 when my life took an unpredictable turn from a broken neck. "It's going to be a long road back from this one," I told myself. I'd broken bones before, but nothing I'd been through could compare to this.

My mom tells this story of what I was like growing up as a kid. Mom says I was a pretty active kid. So active that I broke a few things along the way, like my femur, wrist, and ankle. It was while I was recovering from a broken ankle that the Avon lady paid a visit. She said to my mom, "Michael is doing really well." Perplexed, mom asked, "What do you mean? He can't even walk yet."

"Well, he's out there riding a bike with the other kids," the Avon lady replied. So before I could even walk again, my mom would catch me riding my bike with my cast on or skateboarding with crutches. I just had this attitude that I could do anything. An attitude that has carried me through a lot. With an adventurous spirit and a little accident prone, the hospitals weren't going to go out of business as long as I was around.

But this was more than anything I had faced before. At 18, I was facing the adventure of a lifetime! It was a month before I was to turn 19 years old. I had a job working at a gas station in Lake Forest, California. Wade was my teenage coworker at the gas station. Well, the gas station management had an illegal policy that if the station came up short financially, it would come out of our paychecks. Wade saw a truck turning around and he thought that they pumped $5 worth of gas and were leaving without paying for it. So he asked me to get the vehicles license plate number. I tried but I wasn't able to get the license plate. As it turns out, the truck was just turning around. They didn't pump any gas.

Wade said, "Now I'm going to lose five bucks and it's your fault." I said, "What do you want me to do about it? I tried to get it." "I'm going to fight you," Wade replied. He was a CIF undefeated wrestler. He tackled me with a Full Nelson takedown. With his arm behind my neck, as I hit the pavement, I was instantly paralyzed. I knew I was paralyzed. I knew it that second. I knew there would be a long journey ahead. I assumed it was an accident. So I instantly told Wade that I forgave him, which served me well. I told my sister Cherylin that I knew I had to forgive him if I was going to overcome this situation. But how was an 18 year old able to have the wisdom to know that forgiveness was crucial to my recovery?

A few months before my neck was broken I had been on a spiritual quest that had a profound affect upon me. I wanted to get closer to God. So during the summer of 1981 I decided to climb to the highest mountain I could see. While at the top of the mountain, I planned to fast and commune with God for three days. So off I went to hike to the top of Mt. Baldy. I hitchhiked to the base of Mt. Baldy and decided to hike up to the top of the mountain. I was about halfway up the mountain when it started to get dark. I decided to sleep there on the edge of the mountain. As I lay there, I could see a couple of campfires down below and I could hear the coyotes howl. It was eerie as I drifted off to sleep. The next morning I continued on my trek up the mountain. After several hours of arduous climbing I was almost to the top. I looked up to the peak and saw a small stream trickling down the mountain. "How beautiful," I thought. As I got closer, I realized that it wasn't a stream I was looking at but spider webs along the ground glistening in the sun. I got to the top of the summit and looked at the view from the peak.

Death and destruction. A fire had burned through the area and the whole side of the mountain and valley below was all burned. I felt alone. Abandoned by God. I fell to the ground in tears. "God. Why did you lead me here?" I exclaimed. This is the message I received:

"The climb to the top of the mountain is like the life led for material gain. You work hard your whole life and in the end you have the prize of success. Except it is an illusion like the stream coming from the top of the mountain. In the end, a life spent for the accumulation of material wealth is meaningless and empty. The end of such a life is death and destruction."

It was impressed upon me to go back down the mountain to the river I'd passed on the way to the top. I didn't need to work to get close to God. God was already there. I simply needed to open my heart. So I slid down the side of the mountain and rested by the river under the trees. That trip to the mountain had a profound effect upon me and I knew there was a spiritual purpose to my life. Cue: "Landslide" by Fleetwood Mac:

"I took my love, I took it down

Climbed a mountain and I turned around

And I saw my reflection in the snow covered

hills

'Til the landslide brought it down"

"I can't move. I'm paralyzed." I told Wade. "Call an ambulance." He called an ambulance and they took me to Saddleback Hospital. While in the emergency room, my mom was warned I might not make it through the night.

Dr. Sylvan Palmer, the surgeon, told my parents, "We are going to have to operate blind." Because of my broken neck the blood flow was affected and they wouldn't be able to inject me with dye and take the pictures they normally like to have before an operation like this. The next morning I woke up in a Stryker bed in the ICU. A couple of weeks went by. I was feeling hopeful. I was telling everyone that

I was going to walk again. My doctor stopped by with some bad news.

"You're never going to walk again. You're never going to be able to have children," Doctor Palmer told me.

"No. I'll walk," I told the doctor.

"No, you are NEVER going to walk again," he insisted.

"Watch me!" I proclaimed. The doctors were worried about me. The doctor phoned my mother and he told her that I was never going to walk again. There was too much nerve damage and the gap was too big. He told her not to encourage me. He said I was delusional and that when I finally realized I would never walk again, I would slip into a deep depression. My thinking was that I would walk again. I had to put everything within me into getting better. Another week went by. A friend of the family, Jose Pasqua, an evangelist, came by and prayed for God to heal me. Many people were praying for me. It was around this time that I started to move my left toe. Doctor

Palmer had been reading some of the nurse's comments in my chart.

"What's this about you moving a toe?" he asked.

"I can move my toe," I replied.

"That's a spasm," he informed me.

I looked right at him and said, "No, it's not. I moved it."

Dr. Palmer said he would test my toe. "When I tell you to, move your toe." Then he told me, "Now." I moved my left toe. Astonished, he said do it again when I tell you to.

"Now," he said again. Again I moved my left toe. He brought in another doctor and had me demonstrate again, "Now that you have moved your left toe, the sky's the limit," Dr. Palmer told me.

After that month at Saddleback hospital, I was beginning to move all my extremities. Therapists hooked up devices so I could move my arms and legs without resistance. This wasn't high tech, just boards with ropes attached to a bar above me. I was able to move my left side easier than my right side. The Occupational Therapist at Saddleback wanted me to hold a rolled up cloth in my right hand so eventually it would form a "claw" that would be functional. I refused. I insisted on moving each finger. The finger would be moved for me as I thought and tried to assist with the movement. I was beginning to be able to move, just barely, but it was a beginning. From there I went to Long Beach Memorial Hospital for rehabilitation. While there, I underwent intensive physical therapy, occupational therapy, and hyperbaric oxygen treatment, along with psychological and social therapy. My prognosis leaving the hospital was that I would be wheelchair bound most of the time. I might be able to take a few steps to transfer to a car.

I went home and began going to private physical therapy. I was so lucky that I had a physical therapist with different ideas on what was possible. Studies in the United States claimed you could get nerve regeneration for up to two years; in Europe studies demonstrated that you could continue to improve indefinitely. After two years of physical therapy, I still could not move my right ankle. My private physical therapist, Jacqueline Arie, was a little French woman. She was tough as nails. She swam every day. She'd been through WWII. She was a fighter and she made me be a fighter. She kicked my butt. I worked out at her physical therapy center in Mission Viejo six hours a day, six days a week for four years. I worked every major muscle group each day. Each morning I would think to move my right ankle as I pulled on a rope attached to a cuff on my right ankle and moved it. I kept doing the motion in my mind. I'd say to myself, "Think to move it." I continued to do this exercise each day for two years. After two years, nerves in my right ankle started to fire.

It's interesting. Back then we knew about nerve regeneration but not about how brain reorganization worked. Neuroplasticity or brain plasticity is the ability of the brain to form and reorganize synaptic connection, especially in response to learning to move the body following serious injury. Individual synaptic connections are constantly being removed or recreated. The Hebbian theory goes like this:

"Neurons that fire together, wire together" and "Neurons that fire out of sync, fail to link." It's like meditating on what you intuitively know, what your body is capable of doing. It is faith in action.

Years later I returned to Dr. Palmer's office. The MRI of my neck showed that a huge part of my spine was damaged, like 45 percent no longer functioned. Dr. Palmer brought a colleague to see me after reviewing my MRI. When he came in, I could see the surprise on his face. Because of the extent of the nerve damage, he expected to see someone in an electric wheelchair rather than someone walking with a cane. To what do I attribute my recovery? On a scientific basis, I had extensive nerve damage—and some major nerve regeneration. In addition, my brain reorganized. I demanded my body to work. Everyday. Everyday.

To this day, I still work on that. I tell myself, "Never give up. Never stop." In my next life I'll probably still be working on it. Part of my recovery was nerve regeneration, and part was my brain reorganizing to use the nerves in my spinal cord that are still working. My brain goes, "Left ankle works. We'll use some of the nerves that move the left ankle to move the right ankle." I kept demanding the right ankle to move so my body found a way to move it. I was able to maximize what parts of my spinal cord still work. It's all mind over matter. It's not airy-fairy. It's real. It's a lot of hard work telling my body over and over, "You have to do this."

I physically moved my right ankle as I thought to move it. It's a lot of physical exercise. It's a drain on your brain—this brainwork. Finally, my brain did some reorganization and said, "Okay. I'll move it." So, the reason I am able to move so well with the amount of damage I have to my spinal cord is because I am able to maximize the part of my spinal cord that does work to control my body. From a spiritual perspective, I owe my recovery to God. Like when I'm in ankle pain, I keep a positive attitude. I say, "God is with me." When I'm in pain, I believe God's feeling that pain too. I try to be as strong as I can be so I'm not giving God pain. With each step, God is there taking the step with me. Spirit gives me this will power, which is more than what would come from just me. Doing physical therapy for six hours a day six days a week. What teen would do that? Where did that come from? It came from a Higher Power. Little teenage me could not have done this. Me, in turning it over to God and allowing God to help me was the key. And it wasn't abracadabra. An angel didn't come and tap me with a wand to make me walk. It was a lot of hard work. We have to walk through it. Do the work. You have to open the door to allow it to happen. God can present possibilities and open doors we don't even see. He gave me the strength and wisdom to do what I needed so I could walk again.

Although I took each step, I didn't do it alone. What do I want to do with my life? With this challenge? I want to motivate others. I did some modeling for my friend Katie who owns a spray tan company, Kona Tanning Company. So she took pictures of me getting a spray tan. I was being videotaped and photographed with my cane. A lot of people think they can't follow their dreams. Don't say, "Can't". If you have an illness, injury, or disability, and even if you don't fully recover, don't say, "Can't". Look at me. I am an incomplete quadriplegic and I live a full life. I can ride a bike, snow ski, and scuba dive. I write and play music in a band. I got a degree in biology from UCSC and a teaching credential from UCI. I've been teaching science at a middle school for twenty years. I love working with those kids! And the doctors told me I'd never be able to walk again or have children. Did I mention children? Stay tuned.

I have a service dog named Adele. Before her, I had another service dog, Holly, that I had trained. Holly was getting old so when a friend messaged me that she'd found a dog that had been roaming the streets near a Del Taco in Corona, I had to check her out. I was driving home from Palm Desert and I stopped to see this dog. The dog and Holly liked each other. Since the rescuers had picked her up near a Del Taco, they named her Adele. I loved the name and the dog so we took Adele home with us. We were all together from May until October when Holly got sick with cancer. Now it was just Adele and me. Adele and I worked with a service dog trainer once a week on the weekends for a few hours, and then we would work on the task throughout the week. She's working now and I want to have more training for her. She helps with my stability.

She gets things for me. If I fall, Adele helps me back up. Thank God for Adele's love, help, and dedication to me. I probably fall once a day. I'm a good faller. Really good at falling. I'll have spasms in my ankle that cause me to fall. The spasms I get are difficult to deal with. A couple of weeks ago I had a Botox treatment in my legs to reduce spasms. I already notice that I have no negative side effects like I did with other medications for spasms that make my muscles weak. So far, the Botox is helping.

I've always had a heightened sense of perception—ESP—extra sensory perception. As a scientist, I don't believe in magic. Yet, still, I have it. I contemplate these things. What's going on? For example, a blind person can hear better than the rest of us. When they become blind, do their ears become bigger? Our brain wants input. If a person becomes blind, that part of the brain that was used for sight finds a new purpose. It's dedicated to new senses. For me, half my spinal cord isn't working. Our brain is constantly getting information from our body. We don't consciously notice most of this information. Because of my spinal cord injury, much of the sensory information from my body doesn't make it to my brain. The part of my brain that is no longer receiving information from my body because of the injury doesn't just turn off. It doesn't take a vacation. The brain wants input. If my brain is no longer getting input from my body, it is going to seek other input. So just like a blind person develops better hearing, my brain is more sensitive to extrasensory information. I can feel the energy in my body. I have a heightened sensitivity because a large part of my brain no longer receives information from my body because of the nerve damage in my neck.

I learned to scuba dive when I was sixteen years old. I decided I wanted to become an underwater welder. Scuba was my favorite hobby. So I took welding classes at night at Orange Coast College while in high school. I planned to take hardhat diving course, but my neck injury threw a wrench into my plans. I did go on to get a degree in biology with a major in marine biology from UC Santa Cruz. From there I went on to UC Irvine and received a teaching credential in science.

Children are so innocent. When I was a substitute teacher, I remember walking into a first grade class and being asked, "Why do you walk with a stick?" So I would explain to them in terms first graders could understand why I walk with a "stick". They weren't shy. They hadn't learned that you shouldn't ask someone personal information. My middle school students never asked me about my disability. They don't want to embarrass me. They're trying to be polite. But they do want to know why I walk with a cane. So I tell them, "You can ask me anything." I tell my students what happened and why I walk with a cane. It is harder for me to do my job than it is for a teacher without a disability. Does that mean I don't have do to my work? Because it's harder for me? Is that fair? Guess what? Life isn't fair.

My disability is out there for everyone to see. I walk with a limp, use a cane, and have a service dog. I can't hide it. But we all have challenges we have to face. There are kids who may be facing challenges that we can't see. Maybe there is a student who is slower than other students. So one day the kids start teasing the slower student calling the student a slow poke. What the children didn't know was that the slower person was diabetic and had to be very careful with blood sugar levels. You never know what someone may be going through. Don't bully. Someday, you'll be the person facing a challenge. Because everyone faces challenges at some point. I tell them if they aren't facing any horrible challenges right now, they will. How do I know that? Well, everyone dies. So eventually, someone you love is going to die. Or maybe you will have to deal with your parents getting divorced. Does that mean you don't have to do your homework? There will be times when each of you will have difficulties and some subjects you will have to study harder. It isn't fair, it's just life.

My choice: give it everything you've got. Be kind because you never know what another person is dealing with. If someone is mean to you remember, the best revenge is living a happy life. We all have challenges. Mine is big and it's in-your-face. Seen or unseen, we all have challenges we must face everyday. Every day is full of possibilities. My purpose is to be present in the moment. I impact the lives of about 150 students a year. I impact their lives each day. I don't just teach science. I teach life-coping skills. They get to meet Adele, my service dog. They get to learn how to relate to a disabled person. I love teaching. Students collaborating. It's my own little world. I love science. I love kids. During lunch I don't sit in the teachers lounge. I have lunch in my classroom. Kids come in, even kids who aren't my students. They eat lunch. Some ask me questions or play chess with other students. Some will give treats to Adele. I do the best I can. I try to keep it fun and challenging. Sometimes I succeed. Sometimes I fail. You can't do outstanding things without some failure in the process. I also do a lot outside the classroom. I work out at the gym. I have doctor appointments all the time. Chiropractic treatments and massage. I meditate. I try to balance my life, mentally, emotionally, and spiritually. Try.

After breaking my right ankle and walking on it for a year my doctors decided I needed an operation. A tremendous amount of damage was done to my ankle. So I recently underwent right ankle fusion. Now it looks like I get to put into practice reliance on Spirit for strength each day. Everything is connected. I am never alone. Here we go—learning to walk again. Cue: "Foo Fighters Walk"

"Learning to walk again, I believe I've waited

long enough. Where do I begin?"

As much as I love scuba and science, I also have a passion for writing and playing music. Presently I am writing an album, writing a book, and studying for certificates in Spirituality and Reiki. I'm also learning motivational speaking. This is synchronicity. As things just fall into place, I see God's will. I have been writing music since I was 14 years old. I recently wrote a song that I plan to perform at the Spiritual Center I attend in Mission Viejo: InSpirit. This song just came to me. It's a blues/gospel song, a little on the edgy side. The music and lyrics came so fast I could barely keep up. People were around talking and asking me to do things. It was quite a challenge to keep up. It was like taking dictation. Yet like looking in a mirror, reflecting my life. The title is "I've Been Set Free."

Now. About those grandchildren. The doctors were wrong on two counts. First, they told me I would never walk again. Second, they told me I'd never have children. I have a 25-year-old daughter named Ashleigh. I have two six-year old granddaughters: Ashlynn and Delliah and a one-year old grandson, Tyler Joe.

At age 55, I'm a grandpa to three precious angels. Impossible is just a state of mind. Never give up!

Here's my latest song:

"I've Been Set Free"

I take one step forward, Two steps back

I take one step forward, Two steps back

I take one step forward, Knocked two steps back

Man I'm ready for a major attack!

Devil get behind me, Get outta my way

I'm on a mission and I'm not here to play

Knock me down and you know what I'll do

I got a Power inside that's bigger than you!

Ooo-oo (backup female singers, chorus)

I am not stopping and I'm not turning back.

I'm moving forward. You best step aside.

I'm connected to the Power that fills me inside!

The song and the music go on. Stay tuned for news of my upcoming performance.

"Could a greater miracle take place than for us to look through each other's eyes for an instant?"

Henry David Thoreau

The Hardy Ritsema Story

When I look back on my life I am amazed at the sequence of events that brought me to this time. I'm 82 years old and still thriving. Well, the Parkinson's Disease makes it a bit harder for me to get around, but my wonderful wife of almost 60 years keeps me focused on living life to the fullest. Currently, we live in Laguna Woods Village, California where there are many things to do. We go to an exercise class twice a week for people with Parkinson's. We go to many concerts, like seeing Pat Boone, attend a philosophy class, and are members of the Film Club, the Nifty's Club and the Lecture Series. We play euchre once a week with friends.

On Monday mornings we are at the Senior Center with the Tremble Clef Choir. It's for people with Parkinson's and their caregivers. We all tremble and we all sing under the leadership of Karen Skipper and do concerts at various venues in the area. We've made some good friends in the group and I'm singing better than ever. Besides these activities, we really enjoy going near to the ocean. Dana Point Harbor is a special place where we watch the great blue herons make their nests, walk around the island, watch the waves crash into the rocks by the Ocean Institute, and see and listen to the sea lions that lounge there. But best is the ice cream we treat ourselves with after walking. Yes, we do something every day and love it.

My parents came to this country from the Netherlands. They met in Grand Rapids, Michigan and raised three boys there. As I was growing up my dad would urge me to learn a trade – like carpentry – so that I could earn a living. My first job at the age of nine was working in the produce fields for one dollar a day. Never had I felt so wealthy as when I got my first check for five dollars. I continued this summer employment until I was 15 when I decided that I was above such work. However, on the third day of my self-imposed retirement, my dad indicated otherwise. He told me that if I did not have a summer job by the evening of the next day he would find one for me but he could not guarantee that it would be for money. The next day and every day after, I was back at work in the produce fields.

I went to Wyoming High School and barely passed because I just didn't take education seriously. For a couple years I tried different jobs: construction, detailing cars, etc. At the age of 19 I volunteered to be drafted. I thought I was going to be in the Army but was drafted into the Navy. I spent the next two years aboard the USS Turner DDR 834. After serving two years, I returned to Wyoming, Michigan and began dating my wife-to-be, Kathy Faber. If not for her, I probably would have gone back into the Navy or continued doing construction/concrete work at $1.50 an hour. I remember hearing Kathy's brothers and their friends discussing college, which was beyond my understanding but got my interest. Fairly soon after we got married which was on April 3, 1959, she said, "You should go to college."

In the Fall of 1959, with her blessing and encouragement, I went back to Wyoming High School and spoke with the principal, Mr. Davis. For reasons that will remain unwritten, Mr. Davis had no problem remembering me! In fact when I told him I was interested in going to college, he suggested I fill out an application form he happened to have for Calvin College right then. He said, "Fill out the forms and we will attach your academic records and send everything to Calvin College." Little did I know that an attached note from him was going to make a big difference. Several weeks later I received a note from the dean at Calvin College. His response to my request was: "You are not college material, but based on a note from your high school principal, we are willing to let you attend on probation." My response: FANTASTIC!

I began Calvin in the January semester of 1960. During my years at college, I worked part-time on a surveying crew. Kathy had $10.00 a week to spend on groceries. We ate goat meat from goats that my dad raised and pot pies. (Five for a dollar!) We had a baby girl in diapers and another baby on the way. My wife also gave piano lessons and would stuff envelopes for Calvin College, plus other small jobs. She also tutored me in English grammar and spelling, as those were not my strong points. Through it all no one ever said, "I wish you weren't going to school."

Kathy comes from a unique family. They were and still are caring, giving and serving people. Across the street from her family home in Cutlerville, Michigan was a mental health facility that drew people from around the country. In the reception area was information for anyone who needed a place to stay to come on over to their house and a place would be ready for anyone who needed it. I never knew who or how many people would be there when I would come to pick up Kathy for a date! They came as strangers and left as friends.

During my last year at Calvin College, I decided to become a social worker and I applied to the University of Michigan for graduate school. During my interview at the University, I said I would need a scholarship of some kind. A scholarship from the State of Michigan was granted. Next was arranging for me to finish my exams at Calvin early, as the semester at U of M in January would begin before Calvin ended. The dean at Calvin did make arrangements for this and I took the exams and passed and graduated and started U of M in January of 1964. In June, of 1965, I graduated with my degree and we moved to Saginaw, Michigan to begin working for the State of Michigan as a parole officer for juveniles.

Four months after moving to Saginaw, I ended up in the hospital with extreme pain in my left side. One doctor who checked me thought I would need to have a kidney removed. However, X-rays determined that I had a non-Hodgkin's lymphoma sarcoma growth on the aorta that was inoperable. I had a strong series of radiation treatments that did reduce the tumor completely. I'm 82 and still here!

At work, Saginaw County asked me to assume the responsibility for Child Abuse and Neglect Services. During the next three years I developed and supervised that program. The probate court worked with us on this. We'd recommend foster care or sever parental rights. Sometimes we proposed adoption. Many of these cases inevitably involved court hearings and legal representation. This got me to thinking that maybe I should have been a lawyer. I shared this with Kathy and her response was: "So why don't you go to law school?" So in 1970 we packed up and moved to Detroit.

By now we had three children and looking back on all of this I wonder how we handled it. I enrolled in the Detroit College of Law and attended night school for four years. I also worked full time, as a school social worker for one year. I was laid off from that job and started to look for another one. We had planned a six-week camping trip with our family during the summer, as school was closed and there were no night classes at law school. In June I applied for a job with Wayne County. We left on our camping trip in mid-June not knowing whether or not I had a job. When we got to the Rocky Mountain National Park in Colorado, I found a pay phone and called back to Wayne County and was told that, yes, I was being offered a job and could I start the next week. With some hesitation I said I was in Colorado and had another five weeks of a trip planned. Thankfully, they understood and said I could start as soon as I got back. I worked for the Wayne County Court as a family counselor. After my first year at Wayne County, I became a supervisor in the child support division.

In 1969, after four years of law school at night, I graduated from the Detroit College of Law. In 1970 I passed the Michigan Bar. I continued to work for Wayne County in the child support division. In 1980 I applied and was appointed to the position of Director of the "Friend of the Court" for Wayne County. In Michigan the "Friend of the Court" has existed since 1916. It provides investigation, establishment, and compliance assistance to the court in domestic relations matters. This may include paternity establishment, child support, custody and visitation. The title "Friend of the Court" refers to both the system and to the individual in charge of the system. A law degree was required for this position as attorneys are a part of this organization and represented the interests of the court. This required supervising about 300 employees with various skills and talents. This was also a time when the federal government was pouring money into child support collection efforts. While holding this position, I did numerous presentations at conferences and conventions in many states regarding child support issues. Comparatively speaking, we were very effective at collecting child support. The only regret I have was when I declined an opportunity to give a presentation in Hawaii. I wanted my wife to go with me but she was teaching school and couldn't get off.

During my tenure as "Friend of the Court", I successfully completed the academic requirements for becoming a graduate fellow of the National Institute for Court Management. The awarding of this document was given to me and my classmates at the U.S. Supreme Court in Washington D.C. by Chief Justice Warren Burger. Kathy was able to be with me for this occasion.

I was the director of the Wayne County "Friend of the Court" for 18 years until I retired in 1998 at the age of 62. We then moved to Rockford, Michigan as both our daughters and, especially, our grandchildren lived there. We so enjoyed watching them grow up and being a part of their lives.

About five years ago, in 2013, my family started noticing things – like some excessive drooling, not using my left arm as much and some minor trembling. Sometimes I would stare into space. I was diagnosed with Parkinson's disease and started on medication. It is quite well-controlled and life goes on. Our favorite saying is "I may have Parkinson's but Parkinson's doesn't have me!"

Our faith in God is very important to us. We thank God everyday for this wonderful life. And we are thankful for our family and friends for their love and support.

Our youngest daughter, Suelyn, who had moved to Laguna Nigel, California, encouraged us to move to California so we could be near her, her husband, and their adult children. Our daughter, Pam and husband live in Williamsburg, Virginia and our son, Daniel and his family live in England, as that is where his wife is from. So now we live in Laguna Woods Village and see our daughter frequently.

Sometimes when I reminisce, I think of the ways my wife is like her mother and the influence both had on my life. I didn't know what I wanted to do and encouragement came to me in wonderful ways. Kathy loves to have fun and is very caring. She earned a teaching degree from Wayne State University while I was going to law school, plus raising three children. She then became an elementary school teacher. She went on to earn a Masters Degree at the University of Michigan. After some years of teaching, she became the coordinator of about sixty volunteers for a Hospice program out of Henry Ford Hospital in Detroit.

We have traveled extensively in our lives; including recently taking a seven-day cruise with two other couples of which both men also have Parkinson's Disease. We will be celebrating our 60th wedding anniversary next year. When people ask Kathy about our wedding date, she always says, "Ask Hardy. He knows." She had the numbers 4-3-59 engraved inside my wedding ring. I have no excuse for not remembering. But how could I forget? She's the best thing that ever happened to me!

"Miracles come in moments.

Be ready and willing."

Wayne Dyer

Valley Girl

My name is Rachel. I was born into a loving family in Manhattan, New York on June 21, 1946. When I was five years old my family moved to what was the San Fernando Valley, specifically the part called North Hollywood. That's where I grew up and went to Grant High School. I married at age 19 and went on to get my B.A. in Archaeology. My husband — now my ex-husband — was working on his doctorate in Archeology at the University of Calgary in Calgary, Alberta, Canada, where we both got our degrees. We called our field trips "digs." It was fun and interesting but that's not what I ultimately decided to do.

I'm still a workingwoman. Since 1991, I counsel immigrant felons who are in jail. I help them get approved under the bilateral treaties and Conventions we have with Canada,

Mexico, and many other countries around the world. I'm busy doing this between twenty and thirty hours a week. I see myself as an activist and find this work to be very important. I have marched against the Vietnam War in the '60's. I met my husband during one of those marches. A close family friend was an attorney who went to Mississippi on the voter registration drive to help blacks who got arrested during the Civil Rights movement. And I am still marching/protesting, and on January 21, 2017, I wore a pink "pussy" hat while I attended the Women's March in Santa Ana. Because so many women attended the March we didn't walk very fast and I was fortunate to have a friend that let me lean on her to make my walk easier.

My body has a condition called Huntington's Disease. It's a tough one. It is hereditary. My father had it and one of my brothers tested positive but is still asymptomatic and my other brother is untested but symptomatic. When I began having difficulty speaking clearly, I decided to be tested and diagnosed. I wanted to be in a study group and I thought it would be best for me to start on medication. At this point, I'm not in a study group. I know that, potentially, things could get worse, but I have chosen to have a positive attitude and to keep myself as active and healthy as possible.

Huntington's Disease is a genetic disorder where just one of the over 100,000 genes each human has is abnormal (Chromosome 4). If a parent has this faulty gene, there is a 50-50 chance any offspring will inherit it. Anyone with this gene will eventually develop Huntington's Disease. This flawed gene encodes a protein (Huntintin) that leads directly to the programmed destruction of cells (neurons) deep within the brain.

While symptoms of HD can vary from person to person, cognitive, as well as motor functions suffer. Uncontrollable dance-like body movements (chorea) are sometimes observed in individuals who develop HD as adults. There is no cure, little symptom relief, and as with all disabilities, can continue to deteriorate.

I have a beautiful daughter, Tiffany. She and her husband Shawn are raising their three awesome daughters and my granddaughters. Trinity is 14, Anna 2-1/2, and Olivia is one-year old. They reside in Mesa, Arizona, which isn't too far away. We keep in touch and visit as much as we can. I attend the U.U. Church in Costa Mesa, California. U.U. stands for Unitarian Universalism, which is a liberal religion characterized by a "free and responsible search for truth and meaning." The Unitarian Universalist Church does not have a creed; instead we have a set of seven principles by which we live our lives of service. The U.U.s are unified by their shared search for spiritual growth, which varies among us.

I have a precious little dog named Prince. He wakes me early in the morning and we walk one mile and a quarter every day. For a while I went to a physical therapist but now choose to exercise on my own, keeping in mind what all the exercise gurus tell us: tighten the core. I do all my own cooking and have a very healthy diet. I regularly take vitamins and fish oil for Omega 3. I see my chiropractor at least every six weeks and occasionally see an acupuncturist.

I moved to Laguna Woods Village in 2009 because of the support system and use the bus or Lyft driver to go shopping at my favorite stores: Trader Joe's and Mother's. I like my home to be tidy and clean and have a housekeeper come every two weeks. At the time of this publication, I am in the process of selling my Condo in Laguna Woods and moving to Mesa, Arizona to be closer to my daughter and her family.

Isn't life all about attitude? I think if you have a healthy, positive attitude you live the best life possible and you inspire other people. That's what I hope to do with my story: inspire a few people who have challenges. Know that everything happens for a reason. Stay positive.

That's my advice from this Valley Girl. That's why this Valley Girl is determined to stay positive and to make everyday a good experience.

"Out of difficulties grow miracles."

Jean De La Bruyere

Lorita Braun Brown

In my day, I've been a water-skier, a snow-skier, and an ice-skater. I've sung in nightclubs in Hawaii and, in California at the Admiral Risty Restaurant lounge in Palos Verdes, and in a couple of nightclubs in Florida. I'm an author, a poet, a singer, a wife, and a mom. I've been married to Michael for 33 years and been Michaela's mom for 20 years. One of the books I've written is *Secrets of the Soul* and the other is *New Horizons*.

I have a beautiful black dog named Oliver. He's playful and very energetic, but most of all, he's my faithful companion: my guide dog. He can be frisky, he can be really entertaining but, most of all, he is my loving friend. I maneuver by cane, by sounds, and by facial vision where things bounce off the side of my face. At the movies I use descriptive headsets. I have a talking computer, a talking calculator, a talking alarm clock and my email talks to me. Most of all, I have a husband and a daughter who bring love, light, and helpful companionship into my life. I am blind.

Because mom was but six months into her pregnancy, we spent our first weeks in an incubator. I was born July 17, 1953, with a twin brother. I weighed two pounds and two ounces. I lost my sight because of an overdose of oxygen in my incubator. That used to happen to premature babies; they were blinded. I lived; my brother died. His lungs were weak and underdeveloped. I have two older sisters: Susan and Kristina and had a younger brother Eddie, who died several years ago.

When I was a kid my mom was on the show Queen for a Day. As the winner, she took home furniture, appliances, and some of those Betsy-Wetsy dolls, the ones that drink and wet. Mom was be-robed, crowned, and given two-dozen roses. Of course, the whole family was thrilled. We thought we were famous.

As a kid I was brave, in part, I think, because my mother encouraged me to try new things. When my brother wanted to teach me to ride a bike, mom said, "Yeah, go try it." The first time I water-skied I wasn't sure what to do but as the boat took off and I remained squatted down on the skis, my friend Toni McMorris yelled out, "Get your butt out of the water." So I stood up.

As a blind snow skier I wore a vest that said, "Blind Skier." My guide wore a vest that said, "Brave Guide." One time I slipped while ice-skating and busted my lip but that didn't stop me from trying new things and living life to the fullest.

My husband Michael works for the USPS. He is at work from about midnight until six in the morning, as an electrical technician. My daughter Michaela works nights at Disneyland in Anaheim as a custodian. She aspires to be on Broadway as a singer and a dancer; another entertainer in the family.

I am a firm believer in metaphysics and positive thinking. No trauma drama, no drama queen for me. I've studied the Religious Science philosophy under Rev. Dr. Peggy Basset and Rev. Dr. Jim Turrell for many years. Dr. Ernest Holmes, the founder of Religious Science, began writing books and teaching this philosophy in the 1950's and it keeps me centered, aware, and alert. I also love the metaphysical poets. One of my favorites Tagore Rabindranath wrote: "Where the mind is without fear and the head is held high … into every-widening thought and action … into that heaven of freedom, my Father, let my country awake."

We all have mishaps in our lives and if we can learn to live with an upbeat attitude, we'll conquer our fears and minor annoyances. A few years ago I had a hip replacement, then fell and broke my shoulder. So I reminded myself of Rumi's advice:

"Let yourself be silently drawn by the stronger pull of what you really love. The wound is the place where the Light enters. Don't grieve. Anything you lose comes around in another form."

Rumi is often quoted, "Out beyond ideas of wrong-doing and right-doing there is a field. I'll meet you there."

At this time, my husband and I, along with our daughter and one of her friends are preparing to spend six days at the Disney Aulani Resort on the island of Oahu. I love the islands, especially Oahu and Kauai. I think of Hawaii as my home. My heart belongs to Hawaii. We haven't been there for several years so are looking forward to chilling out, relaxing, maybe shopping.

A Spiritual Matrimony

By Lorita Braun Brown

I collect dreams

As I often collect sand castles

Running endlessly through the fields of life

Freely looking, losing, and finding

Finding a part of me which I never could have

known

Without absence and emptiness

A spiritual matrimony with myself

A soul-searching silence

Which the heart feeds off of

And grows from.

Through the splendors of life comes death

Dressed in its shining armor of love

Black darkness touches every cloud

The definition of being in love

Is

Being peacefully insane.

About the Author

Sue grew up on a little farm in Dominguez Hills, feeding the goats and pigs and chickens, and tending the crops. She likes to tell people, "I went to Compton High and I ain't afraid of nothin'."

She spent thirty years working in Education as a teacher's aide at La Vista in Fullerton, an attendance clerk at Yorba Middle School, and a school district insurance clerk for Orange Unified School District, an English teacher at Anaheim High School and an advisor to Student Teachers at Cal State Fullerton.

After retiring, she discovered Laughter Yoga and gives presentations on the healthy benefits of laughter. She hikes every chance she gets, and works out in a pool exercise class. She is involved in an inter-faith group: S.T.E.P. (Sisters Together Envisioning Peace), facilitates a Caring Circle group in their home once a month, attends services at InSpirit Center for Spiritual Living in Mission Viejo, and visits their three kids, seven grandkids, and eight great-grandkids whenever possible. She tends to their community garden plot, raising olallieberries, tomatoes, zucchini, chard, kale, cucumbers, blueberries, eggplant, and herbs. Recently they were given a fruit plot, which holds a huge apple tree. As a vegetarian, she chops things up in the kitchen almost daily. She organizes food drives at the local market for *South County Outreach*, a fabulous organization whose goal is to prevent homelessness by assisting needy families.

When not busy with these activities, she writes essays and poetry. She is now in the process of finishing up two books: *Miracle People* and *Travels of the King and I*. She and her husband, Richard, love traveling in foreign countries and have traveled around the US in their 2005 Dodge Caravan. In her spare time she's an avid bird-watcher.

For the last five years, they have lived in the Orange County, California retirement community of Laguna Woods Village but it seems Sue has not taken "retirement" seriously.

Acknowledgements

Friends and family members have encouraged me to keep bringing together these stories of people—Miracle People—who inspire us everyday. They constantly remind us to stay positive, to look inward for motivation, to ask for help when needed.

My husband, Richard, who was diagnosed with MS when he was only 18, has been the most inspirational person I've ever met. Kathie and Jack have been dear friends for over 30 years. Lorita we met at a Christmas Party. Rachel, Sam, Hardy, Doug, Dave, live in Laguna Woods Village as our dear neighbors. Michael and his precious Adele we know from InSpirit, our Center for Spiritual Living community. Marilyn is another of our pool buddies. Christina is a part-time villager. Joyce was my student at Anaheim High School. And Eric, who is a constant reminder to look on the bright side, we know through a group of friends we met when we lived in Olde Towne Orange.

I truly feel blessed with the love, the patience, and the courage these Miracle People bring to my life. And, as I often say, "I love my life!"

"I believe in family and friends.
I believe laughter really is the best medicine.
I believe in hugging and in listening
and in writing.
.I believe in the miracle of
persistence when creating a book.
I believe in miracles.
Hey you guys. We did it!"

And so it is.

Made in the USA
Monee, IL
04 May 2023

32907248R00079